SCOOBY-DOO EXPLORES
HABITATS

BY JOHN SAZAKLIS

PEBBLE
a capstone imprint

Published by Pebble, an imprint of Capstone
1710 Roe Crest Drive, North Mankato, Minnesota 56003
capstonepub.com

Library of Congress Cataloging-in-Publication Data is available on the Library of Congress website
ISBN: 9780756576332 (hardcover)
ISBN: 9780756576288 (paperback)
ISBN: 9780756576295 (ebook PDF)

Summary: Scooby-Doo and gang learn about habitats.

Editorial Credits
Editor: Christianne Jones; Designer: Bobbie Nuytten; Media Researcher: Rebekah Hubstenberger;
Production Specialist: Whitney Schaefer

Image Credits
Getty Images: brytta, 15 (top), by Frank Olsen, Norway, 5 (eagle), by Tatsiana Volskaya, 7 (bottom),
danm, 14, Feng Wei Photography, 7 (top), Georgette Douwma, Cover (bottom right), 18, Gerard
Soury, 17 (top right), 19 (bottom), iStock/Alberto Carrera, 17 (middle left), iStock/efenzi, 22,
iStock/quickshooting, 3 (middle right), Jason Edwards, 19 (middle), Jim Cumming, 31 (top), joe
daniel price, 1, Joe Hornbuckle/500px, 11 (middle), John Baggaley, 6, john finney photography, 3
(bottom middle), 12 (bottom), Johner Images, 21 (middle left), Kristian Bell, 11 (bottom), LazyPixel/
Brunner Sébastien, 21 (middle right), Mike Perry - flickr.com/mrperry, 23 (middle), Paul Souders,
5 (top right), 23 (top), Peter Dazeley, 23 (bottom), Picture by Tambako the Jaguar, 5 (snow leopard),
20, Teresa Kopec, 27 (top), 31 (middle), timandtim, 2 (bottom right), 28, Ton Koene photography, 27
(middle), Tui De Roy, 25 (middle left), Vicki Jauron, Babylon and Beyond Photography, 15 (bottom),
29 (top left); Shutterstock: Alexey Seafarer, 25 (top right), aquapix, 17 (middle right), Asmakhan992,
Cover (top right), Been there YB, 9 (middle right), BGSmith, 5 (middle right), Cat Downie, 9 (top
right), CherylRamalho, 8, David Hanlon, 27 (bottom), Dmitry Fch, 15 (middle), ESB Professional,
19 (top), FloridaStock, 13 (top), gregorioa, 7 (middle), Gunter Nuyts, 21 (top right), Hieu-Trung Le,
2 (bottom left), 24, jack-sooksan, 13 (middle), Jason Ashman, 31 (bottom), JoannaPerchaluk, 25 (top
right), kelifamily, 9 (middle), marcin jucha, 29 (top right), MarynaG, 4, Nikita Tiunov, 30, NotionPic,
3, 16, design element (boat), Oleg Kovtun Hydrobio, 9 (left), satit sewtiw, 3 (bottom left), 16, Sean
Xu, 12 (top right), Sopotnicki, 11 (top), Steve Heap, 10, StockPhotoAstur, 29 (middle left), Teo
Tarras, Cover (middle right), Tom Middleton, 25 (middle right), Troutnut, 26

HABITAT HOPPING

Scooby-Doo and Mystery Inc. are hunting for habitats!

A habitat is the home of an animal or plant. Different kinds of animals and plants live in different habitats. Rainforests, deserts, mountains, grasslands, forests, oceans, and tundras are some habitats.

Use the clues in the photos and text to guess which habitat the gang is exploring!

Scooby and Shaggy spot rocks all around them. They see the forest and flowers along a river. It sure is warm down in the valley.

Ruh-roh! They bump into a big brown bear eating breakfast.

The frightened friends run up the rocks. As they get higher, the weather gets colder. They also see snow leopards, bighorn sheep, and eagles.

SCOOBY-DOO, WHERE ARE YOU?

WE ARE IN THE MOUNTAINS!

Like, the view is great at the top, Scoob, but it's all downhill from here.

Rhat's right!

The top of a mountain is called the summit. Mount Everest has the world's highest summit.

Volcanoes are also mountains, but they are formed in a different way.

Mountains cover about 25 percent of the world's land.

Scooby-Doo and his friends leave the mountains and drive over endless dunes of dry sand.

Sunshine from a clear sky beats down on them. Phew, it's hot!

Jinkies! They see a fox chase a kangaroo rat around a prickly plant.

That plant is called a cactus. Instead of leaves, it has sharp, pointy spikes. So, leaf it alone—get the point?

SCOOBY-DOO, WHERE ARE YOU?

WE ARE IN THE DESERT!

The largest hot desert in the world is the Sahara in North Africa. The largest cold desert is Antarctica.

A cactus stores water in its stems. That's how it survives with little rain.

Most desert animals stay underground during the day. They come out to hunt for food at night when it's cooler.

After the desert, the gang visits a place that's not too hot and not too cold.

The temperature is just right to grow tall grass, short grass, and wildflowers.

Jeepers! A bald eagle swoops overhead looking for fish, mammals, and reptiles to eat.

Luckily, that bison over there is too big to be an eagle meal. Speaking of hungry hunters . . .

SCOOBY-DOO, WHERE ARE YOU?

Grasslands have many different names, including savannas, steppes, and prairies.

Grasslands can be found on every continent except Antarctica.

Grasslands in Africa have lions, rhinos, and elephants.

Scooby and Shaggy lead the gang out of the grasslands. They head somewhere open and wet.

The thirsty Great Dane laps up the liquid, but it's too salty. **BLAH!**

A school of spiny dogfish swim past Scoob in a hurry, followed by some rushing redfish.

ZOINKS! A great white shark breaks the surface. **SPLASH!**

SCOOBY-DOO, WHERE ARE YOU?

WE ARE IN THE OCEAN!

Like, do you know what kind of ship never sinks?

Friendship!

The five oceans are the Pacific, Atlantic, Indian, Southern, and Arctic.

About one million species of animals live in the ocean.

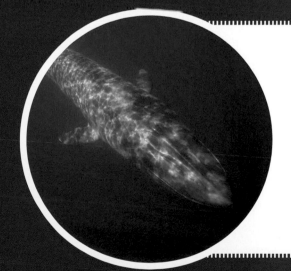

The largest ocean animal is the blue whale.

The Mystery Machine heads from the ocean to a tropical oasis.

Rain falls all around the flora and fauna. Lots of fungus fills the floor.

Groovy! The gang sees gorillas on thick vines through the tall trees.

But beware— poison dart frogs and vampire bats lurk in this lush landscape too!

SCOOBY-DOO, WHERE ARE YOU?

Like, what do you put on gifts in the rainforest?

A rainbow!

22

In some rainforests it rains more than an inch every day!

Thick woody vines, orchids, and bamboo are some rainforest plants.

Over a quarter of all known natural medicines were discovered in rainforests.

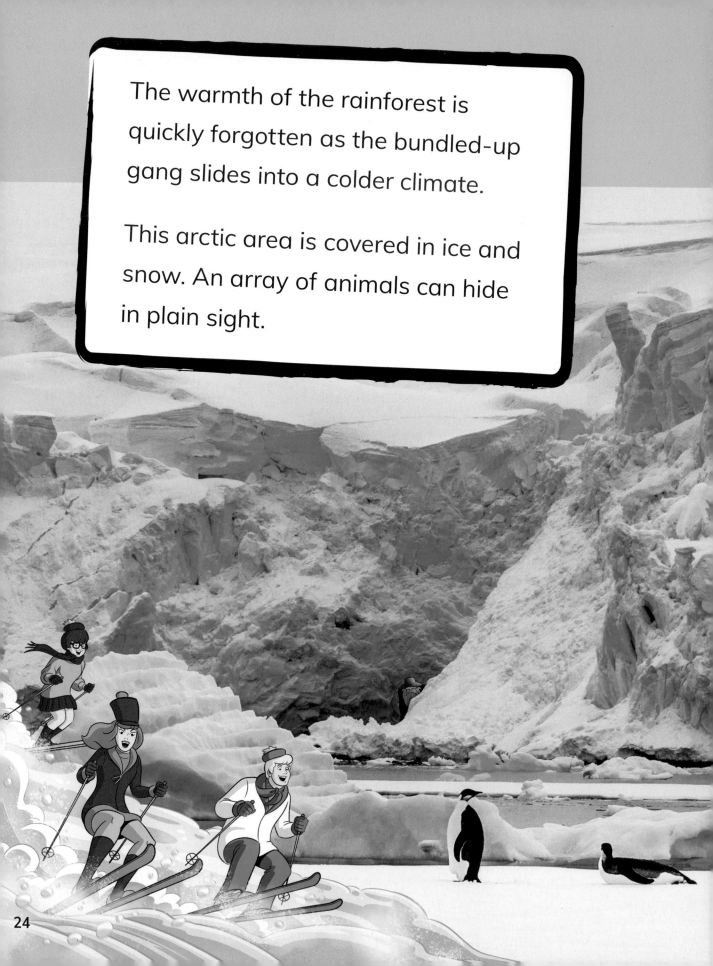

The warmth of the rainforest is quickly forgotten as the bundled-up gang slides into a colder climate.

This arctic area is covered in ice and snow. An array of animals can hide in plain sight.

The bright white fox, polar bear, and snowy owl blend in with the snow.

Few plants can grow in this treeless terrain. But, some moss, grass, and shrubs do grow here.

SCOOBY-DOO, WHERE ARE YOU?

WE ARE IN THE TUNDRA!

Brrr! Like, Scooby's about to become a pup-cicle!

There's "snow" place like home!

The word *tundra* comes from the Finnish word *tunturia*, which means "treeless plain."

The tundra is the coldest habitat. Temperatures are often below zero degrees.

Arctic peoples, like the Inuit, live where they can hunt and fish for food to survive.

From the tundra, Scooby-Doo and his friends arrive at their final destination.

This habitat is home to wild animals and buzzing insects. It also has tons of trees.

PECK! PECK! PECK!

What's that noise? Phew! It's just a woodpecker hunting for bugs.

And look! A deer nibbles on the green undergrowth while a rabbit makes its escape.

SCOOBY-DOO, WHERE ARE YOU?

Forests are home to about 80 percent of the earth's animals and plants.

Forests provide clean air and water for humans as well as animals.

There are more than 60,000 species of trees!

Scooby-Doo and the Mystery Inc. gang traveled to many habitats, but they weren't alone! Miner 49er wanted new habitats to haunt. Look through the book again and find him hiding in each habitat.

ABOUT THE AUTHOR

John Sazaklis is a New York Times bestselling author with almost 100 children's books under his utility belt! He has also illustrated Spider-Man books, created toys for MAD magazine, and written for the BEN 10 animated series. John lives in New York City with his superpowered wife and daughter.